Beginner's Guide To Mental Ray and Autodesk Materials In 3ds Max® 2016

Raavi O'Connor

3ds Max is the registered trademarks of Autodesk Inc.

Book Code: VOO6C

ISBN: 978-1515146711

http://raavidesign.blogspot.co.uk

Contents

Acknowledgements

About the Author

Preface

Section A - Global Illumination, Final Gathering, and Caustics

Section B - Autodesk Materials

Section C - Arch & Design Material

Other eBooks from Raavi Design

This page is intentionally left blank

Acknowledgements

Thanks to:

Sarah O'Connor for the cover art and other promotional material.
Alex for formatting the eBook.
Everyone at Autodesk [www.autodesk.com].

Thanks to all great digital artists who inspire us with their innovative VFX, gaming, animation, and motion graphics content.

And a very special thanks to everyone who helped me along the way in my life and carrier.

Finally, thank you for picking up the book.

This page is intentionally left blank

About the Author

Raavi Design, founded by Raavi O'Connor, is a group of like-minded professionals and freelancers who are specialized in advertising, graphic design, web design and development, digital marketing, multimedia, exhibition, print design, branding, and CG content creation.

At Raavi Design we strive to share the enthusiasm and ideas with other digital artists and provide quality CG content to the aspiring artists and students. Our eBooks are written in an easy to understand language so that the users learn the complex concepts quickly.

The main features of our eBooks are as follows:

* Nicely formatted content in eBooks
* Less theory more practical approach saves you hours of struggle and pain
* Content written in easy to understand language
* Exercises/Labs for practice
* Free updates and exclusive bonus content
* Video tutorials
* Free textures, background design, and 3D files

Here's the list of training eBooks that Raavi has put together:

* The Tutorial Bank: 3D, VFX, & Motion Graphics
* Build Studio Light Setup using 3ds Max and VRay
* Exploring Standard Materials in 3ds Max 2015
* Exploring Standard Materials in 3ds Max 2016
* Exploring Utilities Nodes In Maya 2016
* Create Backgrounds, Textures, and Maps in Photoshop: Using Photoshop CC 2014
* Beginner's Guide To Mental Ray and Autodesk Materials In 3ds Max 2016
* Beginner's Guide For Creating 3D Models In 3ds Max 2016

You can follow **Raavi O'Conner** on Twitter **@raavidesign**.

Why this Book?

This book is aimed at those digital artists who have just started working on the 3ds Max. In this eBook, I have covered Autodesk and mental ray materials. A better understanding of materials and maps gives you ability to add realism to your artwork. The concepts you will learn using this eBook will help you a lot when you will apply shaders and textures to your models.

This book is written in an easy to understand language. The important terms are in bold face so that you never miss them. This book is written using 3ds Max 2016. However, you can use it without a problem with 3ds Max 2015 as well.

What You Will Learn?

You will learn how to use Autodesk and mental ray materials to model realistic looking surfaces. The parameters are explained with examples and related screen captures. Additional tips, guidance, and advice is provided in from of Tips, Notes, and Warnings. You will gain skills by completing the examples provided in the book.

What you need?

To complete the examples in this book, you need v2016 of Autodesk 3ds Max. However, the book is also compatible with the v2015 of 3ds Max. To know more about 3ds Max, visit the following links:

3ds Max: *http://www.autodesk.com/products/3ds-max/overview*

If you are an educator or student, you access free Autodesk software from the **Autodesk Education Community**. The **Autodesk Education Community** is an online resource with more than five million members that lets educators and students to download free Autodesk software. In addition, you can connect with millions of other digital artists to know about latest and greatest in the CG industry.

What are the main features of the eBook?
- Global Illumination, Final Gather, and Caustics explained.
- 9 examples to hone your skills.
- Additional tips, guidance, and advice is provided in from of Tips, Notes, and Warnings.
- Important terms are in bold face so that you never miss them.
- Support for technical aspect of the book.
- 3ds Max files and textures used are available for download.

How This Book Is Structured?

This book is organized to provide you with the knowledge needed to master the standard materials and related maps. This book is divided into three sections:

Section A - Global Illumination, Final Gathering, and Caustics
The mental ray renderer offers two methods for achieving the Global Illumination: photon tracing and final

gathering. This section deals with these two methods as well as the caustics. The example used in the section allow you to grasp the concept explained.

Section B - Autodesk Materials

3ds Max comes with three types of mental ray materials: Autodesk Materials, Arch & Design material, and Special-Purpose mental ray materials. This section deals with the Autodesk materials.

Section C - Arch & Design Material

This section deals with the Arch & Design material. This material is a monolithic material designed to support most of the material that you will use in the architectural and product design renderings. This material is highly tuned for modeling fast glossy reflective and refractive surfaces.

Resources

This eBook is sold via multiple sales channels. If you don't have access to the resources used in this book, you can place a request for the resources by visiting the following link: *http://bit.ly/rd-contact*. Please mention **"Resources - VOO6C"** in the subject line.

Customer Support

At Raavi Design we believe support is personal. Our technical team is always ready to take care of your technical queries. If you have any problem with the technical aspect of the eBook, navigate to *http://bit.ly/rd-contact* and let us know about your query. Please mention **"Technical Query - VOO6C"** in the subject line. We will do our best to resolve your queries.

Reader Feedback

Your feedback is always welcome. Your feedback is critical to our efforts at Raavi Design and it will help us in developing quality titles in the future. To send the feedback, visit *http://bit.ly/rd-contact*. Please mention **"Feedback - VOO6C"** in the subject line.

Errata

We take every precaution while preparing the content of the eBook but mistakes do happen. If you find a mistake in this eBook general or technical, we would be happy that you report it to us so that we can mention it in the errata section of the eBook's online page. If you find any errata, please report them by visiting the following link: *http://bit.ly/rd-contact*. Please mention **"Errata - VOO6C"** in the subject line.

This will help the other readers from frustration. Once your errata is verified, it will appear in the errata section of the book's online page.

Stay Connected

Stay connected with us through Twitter (**@raavidesign**) to know the latest updates about our products, information about books, and other related information.

A-Global Illumination, Final Gathering, and Caustics

Global illumination enhances realism in a scene. In 3ds Max, the **mental ray** renderer offers two methods for achieving the Global Illumination: **photon tracing** and **final gathering**. The primary difference between the two is that the photon tracing works from the light source to the ultimate illuminated target whereas final gathering works from the illuminated object to the light source. You can use these methods separately or combine them for optimal results.

In final gathering, global illumination is established for a point by either sampling a number of directions [rays] over the hemisphere over that point or by averaging a number of nearby final gather points. The orientation of the hemisphere is determined by the surface normal of the triangle on whose surface the point lies. Final gathering is useful when there is slow variations in the indirect illumination in the scene. In film production work, final gathering is the preferred method for indirect illumination. However, for accurate indoor illumination, photon mapping is the preferred method of choice.

Global Illumination

The **mental ray** renderer generates global illumination using the photon mapping technique. In this technique, the **mental ray** renderer traces photons emitted from the light. The photon is traced though the scene. In this process it is reflected and transmitted by objects in the scene. When it hits a diffuse surface, the photon is stored in the photon map. To save the system resources, you need to specify the following:

- Which lights can emit photons for the indirect illumination?
- Which objects can generate caustics or global illumination?
- Which objects can receive caustics or global illumination?

To set these properties, ensure that current renderes is set to mental ray and then RMB click on the object[s] in the scene and then choose **Object Properties** from the **Quad** menu. Set the options in the **Object Properties dialog | mental ray panel | Caustics and Global Illumination [GI] section**. The **mental ray** renderer saves photon maps as PMAP files. In order to use the global illumination in 3ds Max, the photons must bounce through two or more surfaces. When you use photon maps, you might see some artifacts in the renders such as dark corners or variations in lighting, you can eliminate those artifacts by turning on the final gathering.

Example 1: Global Illumination
Let's explore the global illumination settings:

Start 3ds Max and reset it. From the **Customize** menu, choose **Unit Setup** and then in the **Unit Setup dialog | Display Unit Scale group**, select **Metric**. Select **Meters** as units and then click **OK**. Create a box in the scene. Go to the **Modify** panel and set **Length** to **4**, **Width** to **4**, and **Height** to **2**. Convert box to **Editable Poly** and then delete the front face [see Figure 1].

Select all polygons and flip them. Create a **Multi-Subobject** Material and assign it to the box. Create three sub-materials [**Standard** materials] and then assign them red, blue, and green colors, respectively. Connect them to the **Multi-Subobject** material. Create polygon IDs for polygons and assign the **Multi-Subobject** material to the box [see Figure 2]. Create a **Teapot** inside the box.

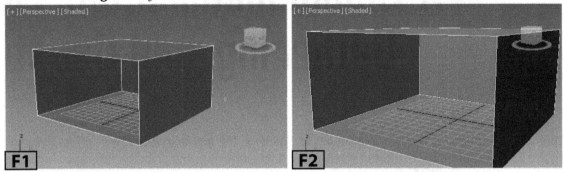

Open the **Render Setup** dialog. Change renderer to **mental ray**. In the **Global Illumination panel | Final Gathering (FG) rollout | Basic section**, turn off **Enable Final Gather**. Create a **mr Area Omni** light inside the box and turn on **Ray Traced Shadows**. Now, take a test render the scene is being illuminated by the direct light coming from the **mr Area Omni** light [see Figure 3]. On the **Render Setup dialog | Global Illumination panel | Caustics & Photon Mapping (GI) rollout | Photon Mapping (GI) group**, turn on **Enable**. This allows the **mental ray** renderer to calculate the global illumination. Set **Maximum Num. Photons per Sample** to **1** and take a test render [see Figure 4]. You will see that effect of individual photons in the render.

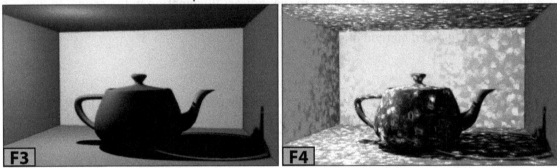

This setting lets you define the number of photons used to compute the intensity of the global illumination. When you increase the value for this control, the result becomes less noisy but more blurry. The larger the sample value is, more time it will take to render.

Set **Maximum Num. Photons per Sample** to **200**. Turn on **Maximum Sample Radius**. Leave the value at **0.025** and take a test render [see Figure 5]. This value sets the size of the photons. When **Maximum Sample Radius** is off, each photon is calculated to be **1/10** of the radius of the full scene. Set **Maximum Sample Radius** to **0.1** and take a render [see Figure 6].

You will see that the photons are blending with each other. Generally, **1/10th** of the scene produces good result. When photons overlap, **mental ray** uses sampling to smooth them. Increasing the value for **Maximum Num. Photons per Sample**, produces smooth result.

Set **Maximum Sample Radius** to **1** and take a test render [see Figure 7]. You will see that on increasing the radius the photons are blending well with each other. Set **Maximum Sample Radius** to **0.1** and turn on **Merge Nearby Photons (saves memory)** and set its spinner to **0.85** and take a test render [see Figure 8].

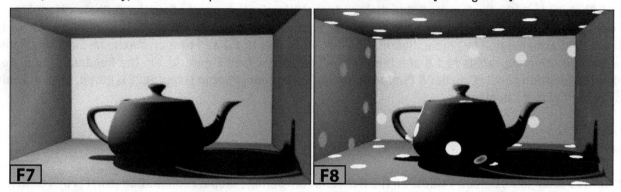

You will see the dots in the render. These settings allows you to set the distance threshold below which **mental ray** merges photons. It reduces the memory requirements for rendering the global illumination.

The **Optimize for Final Gather (Slower GI)** control allows photons to store additional information about how bright its neighbors are. This option is very useful when you want to combine global illumination with final gathering. It allows the final gather to quickly determine how many photons exists in a particular region. It helps in reducing the rendering time.

Turn off **Maximum Sample Radius** and **Merge Nearby Photons (saves memory)**. **Set Maximum Num. Photons per Sample** to **500**.

The controls in the **Trace Depth** group allow you to set the limits for calculating reflections and refractions. These controls refers to the photons used by caustics and global illumination. **Max Depth** control limits the combination of reflection and refraction. **Max. Reflection** controls the number of times a photon can be reflected whereas the **Max. Refractions** controls the number of times a photon can be refracted.

The options in the **Light Properties** group control how lights affect the global illumination. By default, these settings apply to all lights in the scene. You can control per light settings from the light's **mental ray Indirect Illumination** rollout. **Average Caustic Photons per Light** controls the number of photons emitted by each light for use in caustics. Increasing this setting increases the quality of caustics but it also increases the render time. **Average GI Photons per Light** allows you to specify the number of photons emitted by each light for global illumination. **Decay** controls the how the photon's energy decays as photon moves away from the source. If you set this value to **0**, the energy does not decay and photon illuminates the whole scene. The value **1** for **Decay**, decays the energy at the linear rate proportionally to its distance from the light. The value **2** decays the energy at inverse square rate which is how energy decays in the real world.

When **All Objects Generate & Receive GI and Caustics** is on, all objects in the scene can generate and receive caustics and global illumination, regardless of their local object properties settings. When off, **mental ray** respects the object's local properties.

Select the omni light in a viewport and go to the **Modify** panel. On the **mental ray Indirect Illumination** rollout, **Automatically Calculate Energy and Photons** is on. As a result, **mental ray** uses the global light settings for indirect illumination, rather than local settings.

The **Energy, Caustic Photons,** and **GI Photon** controls are global multipliers. **Energy** multiplies the global energy value. **Caustic Photons** multiplies the global Caustic Photons value to increase or decrease the count of photons used to generate caustics by this particular light. **GI Photons** multiply the global GI Photons value to increase or decrease the count of photons used to generate global illumination by this particular light. When **Automatically**

Calculate Energy and Photons is off, the **Manual Settings** group is active. You can use the controls in this group to set various energy and photon values.

Set **GI Photons** to **3**. On the **Render Setup dialog | Global Illumination panel | Caustics & Photon Mapping (GI) rollout | Photon Mapping [GI] group**, the **Multiplier** control allows you to set the intensity and color of the indirect light accumulated by global illumination. Set **Multiplier** to **1.2** and turn on **Maximum Sampling Radius**. Now, set the sampling radius to **1.5** and then take a test render [see Figure 9]. On the **Render Setup dialog | Global Illumination panel | Caustics & Photon Mapping [GI] rollout | Photon Mapping [GI] group**, turn off **Enable** to switch off global illumination.

Example 2: Final Gather

Now, let's see how the final gathering works.

Set **mr Area Omni** to its default values. On the **Render Setup dialog | Global Illumination panel | Final Gathering (FG) rollout**, turn on **Enable Final Gather** and take a test render [see Figure 10].

Multiplier controls the intensity and color of the indirect accumulated light. If you anchor the slider on the **FG Precision Presets** group to the extreme left, the final gathering will be turned off. The default presets are **Draft, Medium, High, Very High,** and **Custom.**

The options in the drop-down below this slider allows you to minimize flickering in the renders. The flickering may appear if you render an animation with a still or moving camera. Use the **Project FG Points From Camera Position** option when camera is not moving and **Project Points from Positions Along Camera Path** when the camera is moving. If the scene contains a fast moving camera, you might achieve better results by using the **Final Gather Map** feature. In this method, map is generated for each frame.

If you use the **Project Points from Positions Along Camera Path** option, **Divide Camera Path by Num. Segments** becomes active. This control allows you to set number of segments into which to divide the camera path. It is recommended that you set at least **1** segment per **15** or **30** frames. If you increase the number of segments make sure that you also set the set **Initial FG Point Density** higher. The value depends on scene contents, and lighting.

Set **Initial FG Point Density** to **0.5**. **Initial FG Point Density** is a multiplier for the final gather points. It increases the number of final gather points in the scene. Set **Rays per FG Point** to **100**. **Rays per FG Point** controls how many rays are used to compute illumination in final gather. This controls helps in removing noise from the renders. Higher values increase render time.

Interpolate Over Num. FG Points defines the number of final gather points that are used for an image sample. For each final gather point, **mental ray** averages indirect light values over the nearest final gather points defined by this control. Increasing this value produces smooth results but increases the render time.

Set **Diffuse Bounces** to **2** and take a test render [see Figure 11]. You will see that there is more color bleed in the render.

Diffuse Bounces sets the number of times **mental ray** calculates the diffuse light bounces for each diffuse ray. This control is affected by **Max Depth. Weight** controls the relative contribution of the diffuse bounces to the final gather solution. The value ranges from **0** [using no diffuse bounces] to **1** [use full diffuse bounces]. Set **Diffuse Bounces** to **0**.

The options in the **Noise Filtering [Speckle Reduction]** drop-down allow you to apply a median filter using the neighboring final gather points. The options are **None, Standard, High, Very High,** and **Extremely High.** The default method is **Standard.** These values make the illumination of the scene better at a cost of rendering time.

The **Max. Depth, Max. Reflections,** and **Max. Refraction** options are already discussed in the global illumination section.

Tip: Noise Filtering
*In the low light scenes, setting **Noise Filtering** to **None** can enhance the overall illumination of the scene.*

When **Use Falloff (Limits Ray Distance)** is on, you can limit the length of the light rays used for regathering using the **Start** and **Stop** controls. This feature can help in reducing the render time in those scenes which are not fully enclosed by geometry.

The controls in the **FG Point Interpolation** group provide access to the legacy method of final gather point interpolation.

FG and GI Disc Caching
Calculating final gather and photon maps required lots of time and calculations. You can save a great deal of rendering time by caching the calculations. It is very useful in situations such as adjusting the camera or re-rendering an animation. The controls in the **Reuse (FG and GI Disk Caching)** rollout are used to generate and use the final gather map [**FGM**] or photon map [**PMAP**] files. You can also use these options to reduce or eliminate flickering in the rendered animations by interpolating among the map files.

For FGM files either you can write all final gather points to a single map file or generate separate files for individual animation frames. When you have separate FGM files for each frame, you can interpolate among them to get a smooth flicker free result.

The drop-down in the **Mode** group lets you choose the method by which 3ds Max generates the cache files. There are two options available: **Single File Only (Best for Walkthrough and Stills)** and **One File Per Frame (Best for Animated Objects).** When **Calculate FG/GI and Skip Final Rendering** is on, 3ds Max performs the final gather and global illumination calculations but does not perform the actual rendering.

The controls in the **Final Gather Map** and **Caustics and Global Illumination Photon Map** let you set the method of writing final gather or photon map cache to the files. The **Interpolate Over N Frames** control lets you set the number of **FGM** files before and after the current frame to use for interpolation.

Caustics
Caustics are the effects of light cast via reflection or refraction through an object. The caustics are calculated using the photon map technique. To render with caustics you need to enable **Caustics** in the **Render Setup Dialog**

| **Global Illumination panel | Caustics & Photon Mapping [GI] rollout | Caustics group**. The **Multiplier** control and color swatch can be used to change the intensity and color of the indirect light accumulated by caustics.

Maximum Num. Photons per Sample sets the number of photons that are used to compute the intensity of the caustics. On increasing this value, **mental ray** produces less noisy [more blurry] caustics. It is recommended that you start with a value of **20** and then increase the value later for final rendering.

Turning on **Maximum Sampling Radius** allows you to set the size of the photons. When this option is unchecked, each photon is calculated to be **1/100** of the radius of the full scene and this settings usually produces good results.

The **Filter** drop-down lets you choose a method for sharpening the caustics. The default method is **Box** which takes less time to render. The **Cone** method makes the caustics sharper. The **Gauss** method produces smoother results than the **Cone** method. **Filter Size** defines the sharpness of the caustics when you work with the **Cone** filter method. On decreasing this value makes caustics sharper, but also slightly noisier. When **Opaque Shadows when Caustics Are Enabled** is on, shadows are opaque, else they may appear partially transparent.

The Last Word

In this section, I've explained about the global illumination, final gathering, and caustics. You can use any method or both to generate indirect light in the scene. Now, you have better understanding of the indirect illumination methods used with **mental ray** in 3ds Max. This knowledge will help you, when you will learn about materials in the next two sections and when you will render objects on which these materials will be applied. In the next section, you will learn about the Autodesk Materials.

B-Autodesk Materials

3ds Max comes with three types of **mental ray** materials: **Autodesk Materials**, **Arch & Design** material, and **Special-Purpose mental ray** materials. **Autodesk Materials** are used to model commonly used surfaces in the construction, design, and the environment. These materials correspond to the materials found in other Autodesk products such as **Autodesk AutoCAD** and **Autodesk Inventor**. So, if you work between these applications, you can share surface and material information among them.

Autodesk Materials are based on the **Arch & Design** material. These materials work best when you use them with physically accurate lights such as photometric lights in a scene, modeled in the real-world units. However, the interface of the **Autodesk Materials** is much simpler than the **Arch & Design** material, therefore, you can achieve good results in less time using **Autodesk Materials**.

Exploring Autodesk Materials

Many of the **Autodesk Materials** use **Autodesk Bitmaps**. The **Autodesk Bitmap** is a simple bitmap type. This bitmap type always uses the real-world mapping coordinates. Therefore, if you have applied a **UVW Map** modifier to any geometry, make sure you turn on **Real-World Map Size** on the **Parameters** rollout. You can also change the default bitmap assignment.

Warning: Autodesk Bitmap compatibility
*3ds Max allows you to disconnect a bitmap, or replace it with another map. However, if you disconnect an **Autodesk Bitmap** in other application such as **Autodesk AutoCAD**, you won't be able to read the **Autodesk Material**. If you are using other applications, make sure that you do not replace the bitmap with a map that only 3ds Max understands.*

Warning: Autodesk Material Library
*If you uninstall or remove Autodesk material library, the materials will no longer will be available for other Autodesk products such as **AutoCAD**, **Revit**, or **Inventor**.*

Autodesk Ceramic

You can use this material to model the glazed ceramic material including porcelain.

Open **autoMat_begin.max**. Open the **Slate Material Editor**. On **Material/Map Browser | Materials | mental ray**, double-click on **Autodesk Ceramic** to display the material's interface in the active view [see Figure 1]. Double-click on the material's node in the active view. In the **Material Editor | Ceramic rollout**, ensure that **Ceramic** is selected as **Type**. The **Ceramic** type produces look of earthenware.

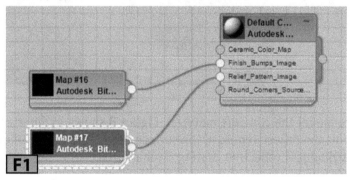

Apply the material to teapot in the scene and take a test render [see Figure 2]. On the **Ceramic** rollout, set **Type** to **Porcelain**. Click **Color** swatch and change color to **blue**. **Color** sets the color of the material. The other two options available for the **Color** control are **Use Map** and **Color By Object**. The **Use Map** option allows you to assign a map to color component of the material. If you set **Color** to **Color By Object**, 3ds Max uses the object's wireframe color as the material color. The **Finish** control lets you adjust the finish and reflectivity of the material.

Note: Color by object
When you use this option, the color appears on rendering but not in the viewport or material previews.

Make sure **Finish** is set to **High Gloss / Glazed** and take a test render [see Figure 3].

Make sure **Finish** is set to **Satin** and take a test render [see Figure 4]. Make sure **Finish** is set to **Matte** and take a test render [see Figure 5]. Now, set **Finish** to **High Gloss / Glazed**.

On the **Finish Bumps** rollout, check **Enable** and make sure **Type** is set to **Wavy** and **Amount** to **0.3**. Now, take a test render [see Figure 6]. The options in the **Finish Bumps** rollout can be used to simulate the patterns that appear in glaze during firing. You can also create custom bumps by using the **Custom** option from the **Type** drop-down. **Amount** sets the strength of the pattern to apply.

On the **Finish Bumps** rollout, turn off **Enable**. On the **Relief Pattern** rollout, turn on **Enable**. Click the **Image** button. On the **Parameters** rollout, click **Source None** button. Select **patten.jpg** from the **Select Bitmap Image File** dialog and click **Open**. On the **Relief Pattern** rollout, set **Amount** to **1.2** and take a test render [see Figure 7]. The options in the **Relief Pattern** rollout allow you to model a pattern stamped into the clay. **Amount** controls the height of the relief pattern.

Autodesk Concrete
This material allows you to model the concrete material. Figure 8 shows its interface. The **Sealant** control of the **Concrete** rollout, controls the reflectiveness of the surface. **None** [see Figure 9] does not affect the surface finish. **Epoxy** [see Figure 10] adds a reflective coating on the surface whereas **Acrylic** [see Figure 11] adds a matte reflective coating.

The **Type** control in the **Finish Bumps** area allows you to set the texture of the concrete. **Broom Straight** which is a default type, specifies a straight broom pattern [see Figure 12]. **Broom Curved** uses a curving broom pattern [see Figure 13]. **Smooth** creates a pattern with speckled irregularities [see Figure 14].

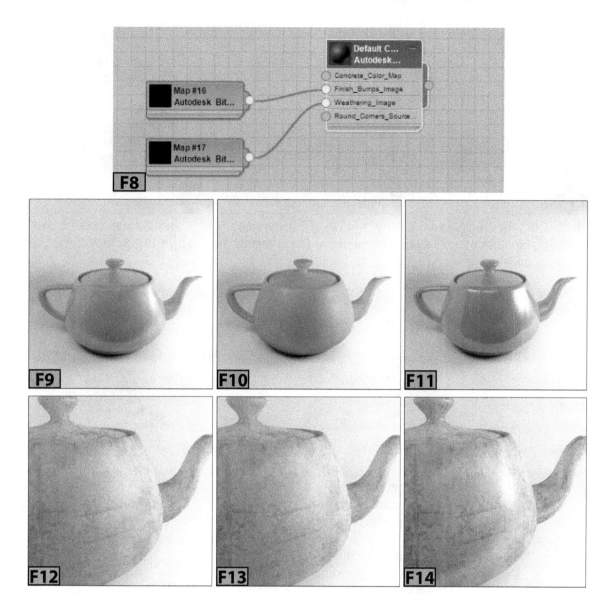

Polished uses a completely smooth pattern [see Figure 15]. You can use **Stamped/Custom** allows you to specify a bitmap for generating the pattern [see Figure 16].

Weathering applies a slight variation in the brightness on the surface of the concrete. The default weathering method is **Automatic** that applies weathering automatically. You can use **Custom** to specify a custom weathering pattern.

Autodesk Generic

This material provides a generic interface for creating a custom appearance. You can convert an Autodesk material to the **Autodesk Generic** material by RMB clicking on the node in the **Slate Material Editor | Active View** and then choosing **Copy as Generic** from the popup menu.

Autodesk Glazing

This material allows you to model a thin and transparent material such as glazing in windows and doors. The **Color** control in the **Glazing** rollout lets you choose the color for the sheet of glass. Figure 17 shows the teapot rendered with the **Blue Green** color applied to it.

Autodesk Harwood

This material is used the model the appearance of a wood. The **Stain** control in the **Wood** rollout allows you to choose a stain to add to the base harwood pattern. Figure 18 shows the wood material with **Brown Stain** color.

The **Finish** control lets you choose the surface finish of the harwood. The **Glossy Varnish** is the default option [see Figure 18]. The other options available are: **Semi-Gloss Varnish** [see Figure 19], **Satin Varnish** [see Figure 20], and **Unfinished** [see Figure 21].

The **Used For** control lets you adjust the appearance of the wood. **Flooring** uses an ocean shader that adds a slight warp to the large surfaces, improving the realism. When you choose **Furniture**, the surfaces are not warped. However, you can use the **Relief Pattern** map to achieve various effects.

When you check **Enable** in the **Relief Pattern** rollout, **mental ray** generates a relief pattern like bump map on the wood surface. The **Type** control lets you choose the relief pattern. When you choose **Based on Wood Grain**, it generates a relief pattern based on the image map used to create the wood pattern. **Custom** allows you to choose a custom map for the relief pattern. **Amount** lets you adjust the height of the relief pattern.

Autodesk Masonry/CMU
This material can be used to model masonry or concrete masonry units [**CMUs**]. Figure 22 and 23 shows the brick and CMU material.

Autodesk Metal

You can use this material to model various metallic surfaces. The **Type** control in the **Metal** rollout lets you choose the type of material you want to create. These materials define the base color and texture of the material. Figure 24 show the brass material. The **Finish** control lets you choose the surface finish for the surface. Figures 24 and 25 show the brass material with the **Polished** and **Brushed** finish, respectively.

Autodesk Metallic Paint

This material allows you to model a metallic paint surface such as paint of a car [see Figure 26].

Autodesk Mirror

This material lets you model a mirror material [see Figure 27].

Autodesk Plastic/Vinyl

This material allows you to model the surfaces that have a synthetic appearance such as plastic or vinyl [see Figures 28 and 29].

Autodesk Point Cloud Material

This is a special purpose material that is automatically applied to any point-cloud object in the scene. This material allows you to control the overall color intensity, ambient occlusion, and shadows.

Autodesk Solid Glass

This material allows you to model the appearance of the solid glass [see Figure 30].

Autodesk Stone

You can use this material to create the appearance of the stone [see Figures 31 and 32]. The **Type** control in the **Finish Bumps** rollout lets you specify the bump pattern. Available options are: **Polished Granite**, **Stone Wall**, **Glossy Marble**, and **Custom**.

F29 F30 F31

Autodesk Wall Paint

This material can be used to model the appearance of a painted surface such as paint on the walls of a room [see Figures 33 and 34]. The **Application** control in the **Wall Paint** rollout lets you choose the texture method. In other words, you can control how paint is applied on the surface. **Roller** is the default method. Other two methods are **Brush** and **Spray**.

F32 F33 F34

Autodesk Water

This material can be used to model appearance of a water surface [see Figure 35]. The **Type** control in the **Water** rollout lets you choose the scale and texture of the water.

The available options are **Swimming Pool, Generic Reflective Pool, Generic Stream/River, Generic Pond/Lake,** and **Generic Sea/Ocean**.

The **Color** control lets you specify the color of the water. This option is only available for **Generic Stream/River, Pond/Lake,** and **Sea/Ocean**.

The following options are available for adjusting the color of the water: **Tropical, Algae/Green, Murky/Brown, Generic Reflecting Pool, Generic Stream/River, Generic Pond/Lake, Generic Sea/Ocean** and **Custom**.

F35

The Last Word

This section introduced you to the **Autodesk Materials**. These materials give you ability to quickly model materials for any type of surface in your scene. In the next section, you will learn about the **Arch & Design** material which is base for all **Autodesk Materials** that you have seen in this section.

C-Arch & Design Material

The mental ray **Arch & Design** material is a specialized material that allows you to create physically accurate renderings. It is designed to support most of the materials used in the architecture and product design renderings. This material includes self-illumination, ambient occlusion, and advanced options for reflectivity and transparency. It can also round off the sharp corners and edges as a render effect. It is especially fine-tuned for fast gloss reflections and refractions thus improving the workflow and performance.

The **Arch & Design** material has built-in description for all important controls. You can view the details in form of a tooltip. To view the tooltip, hover the cursor over a control's spinner, color swatch, checkbox, and so forth.

The **Arch & Design** material attempts to be physically accurate and it outputs a high dynamic range. The visual appeal of the material depends on how colors inside the renderer are mapped to colors displayed on the screen. When you are using the **Arch & Design** material, it is recommended that you use an exposure control such as the **mr Photographic Exposure Control**.

When using the **Arch & Design** material, make sure that you use atleast one of the two methods used with mental ray for indirect illumination: **Final Gathering** or **Global Illumination**. For best results, you can combine final gathering with global illumination. Also, it is recommended that you use physically accurate lights such as **Photometric Lights** with the **Arch & Design** material.

To create an **Arch & Design** material, press **M** to open the **Slate Material Editor**. On the **Material/Map Browser | Materials | mental ray rollout**, double-click on **Arch & Design**. The material's interface is displayed in the active view [see Figure 1]. Figure 2 shows a render of teapot with the default **Arch & Design** material applied to it.

Example 1: Creating the Leather Material
Let's start by creating a leather material [see Figure 3] using the **Arch & Design** material.

Here's is the procedure:

Open **archDefMat.max**. Save the scene with the name **leatherMatEnd.max**. Press **M** to open the **Slate Material Editor**. On the **Material/Map Browser | Materials | mental ray rollout**, double-click on **Arch & Design**. Apply the material to the teapot in the scene. On the **Parameter Editor | Templates rollout**, choose **Pearl Finish** from the drop-down.

Pearl Finish creates soft blurry reflections without affecting colors or maps. **Matte Finish** allows you to simulate an ideal **Lambertian** shading without affecting the colors or maps. **Glossy Finish** lets you simulate strong reflections without affecting colors or maps.

On the **Main material parameters** rollout, click **Color's** button. On the **Material/Map Browser | Maps | Standard rollout**, double-click **Bitmap**. On the **Select Bitmap Image File** dialog, choose **brownLeather.jpg**. On the **Gamma** section of the dialog, choose **Override** and set the spinner next to it to **2.2** and then click **Open**.

Tip: General Maps Rollout
*You can also assign a diffuse map on the **General Maps** rollout.*

Color controls the color of the surface in direct light. **Diffuse Level** allows you to control the brightness of the diffuse color component. **Roughness** controls the blending of the diffuse component into the ambient component. The **Roughness** values ranges from **0** to **1**. At the **0** value, classical **Lambertian** shading is used. Higher values creates more powdery look.

Tip: Gamma 2.2 Setup
*To know more about **Gamma 2.2** setup in 3ds Max, visit the following link:*
http://bit.ly/linear-gamma.

The **Arch & Design** material is energy conserving therefore the actual diffuse level used depends on the reflectivity and transparency. This material makes sure that **diffuse+reflection+refraction** is less than equal to **1**. The incoming light energy is properly distributed to diffuse, reflection, and refraction components so that it maintains the first law of thermodynamics. If you add reflectivity, the energy must be taken from somewhere, therefore the diffuse and transparency component will be reduced accordingly.

The rules for the energy are as follows:

- **Transparency** takes energy from the diffuse color. If you set transparency to **100%**, there will be no diffuse color.
- **Reflectivity** takes energy from diffuse and transparency, therefore, **100%** reflectivity means there is no diffuse color or transparency on the surface.
- **Translucency** is a type of transparency. The **Translucency Weight** parameter defines the percentage of transparency versus translucency.

On the **brownLeather.jpg | Coordinates** rollout, set **U** and **V** to **0.6** in the **Tiling** column. Also, set **Blur** to **0.2** and take a test render [see Figure 4].

On the **Special Purpose Maps** rollout of the material, click **Bump's None** button. On the **Material/Map Browser | Maps | Standard rollout**, double-click **Bitmap**. On the **Select Bitmap Image File** dialog, choose **brownLeather_bump. jpg**. On the **brownLeather_bump.jpg | Coordinates** rollout, set **U** and **V** to **0.6** in the **Tiling** column. Also, set **Blur** to **0.2**. On the **Special Purpose Maps** rollout of the material, set **Bump** to **0.1** and take a test render [see Figure 5].

You can use the **Bump** map button to assign a bump map. The strength of the bump can be adjusted using the spinner located on the left of the button. If you turn on **Do not apply bumps to the diffuse shading**, bumps are applied to all components except the diffuse.

On the **Main material parameters** rollout, turn off **Fast (interpolate)** to generate more accurate glossiness.

When **Fast (interpolate)** is on, a smoothing algorithm is used that allows rays to be reused and smoothed. As a result, you get faster and smoother glossy reflections at a cost of accuracy.

When **Highlight + FG only** is turned on, actual rays are not traced in the scene. Only highlights are shown. In addition to this, soft reflections are shown that are produced by final gathering. You can use this option on surfaces that are less essential in the scene. This option works well with surfaces having weak reflections and blurred glossy reflections.

Tip: Flat surfaces
This method works well with flat surfaces.

Metal material sets the color of reflection cast by the metallic materials. When **Metal material** is on, the **Diffuse Color** control defines the color of reflections. The **Reflectivity** control sets the weight between the diffuse reflections and metallic reflections. When off, the **Reflection Color** control defines the color. The **Reflectivity** control plus **BRDF** settings define the intensity and color of the reflections.

Set **Glossiness** to **0.3**. **Glossiness** controls the sharpness of refraction/transparency. The values ranges from **0** [extremely diffuse or blurry transparency] to **1** [completely clear transparency].

Set **Reflectivity** to **0.2** and take a test render [see Figure 6].

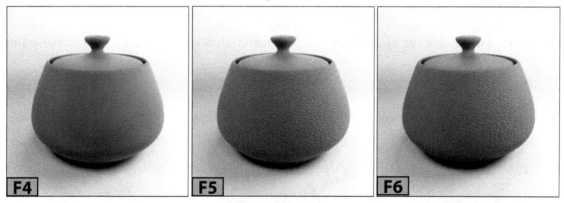

Reflectivity controls the overall level of reflectivity. The reflectivity and color values, also known as specular highlight, define the level of reflections and its intensity. **Glossy Samples** specifies the number of rays [samples] mental ray shoots in order to calculate the glossy refraction. Higher values produce smooth result at a cost of render time.

Tip: Glossy Samples
A value of 32 is enough for most renderings. If you set Glossy Samples to 1, only one ray is shot, regardless of the actual value of Glossiness. It boots the rendering performance. You can use it for your test renderings.

Reflectivity controls the overall level of reflectivity. The reflectivity and color values, also known as specular highlight, define the level of reflections and its intensity. **Glossy Samples** specifies the number of rays [samples] **mental ray** shoots in order to calculate the glossy refraction. Higher values produce smooth result at a cost of render time.

On the **BRDF** rollout, make sure **Custom Reflectivity Function** is selected and then set **0 deg. refl** to **0.2** and **Curve shape** to **2**. Now, take a test render [see Figure 7].

BRDF stands for **Bidirectional Reflectance Distribution Function**. In the real world, the reflectivity of the surface is dependent on the view angle. **BRDF** function allows you to control the reflectivity of the surface based on the angle it is viewed. In real world surfaces such as glass, water, and other dielectric materials with **Fresnel** effects, the angular dependency of reflection is dependent on **IOR** or **index of refraction**. The **Arch & Design** material allows you to set the angular based reflectivity values using **0-degree faces** [surfaces directly facing the camera] and **90-degree faces** [surfaces 90 degrees to the camera]. **Curve Shape** controls the falloff of the **BRDF** curve. When you choose **By IOR [fresnel reflections]**, the reflectivity is entirely guided by the material's index of refraction.

On the **Fast Glossy Interpolation** rollout, set **Interpolation grid density** to **1 (same as rendering)** and take a test render [see Figure 8].

Warning: Interpolation

Interpolation *can cause artifacts because it is calculated on low res grid. It can also cause oversmoothing as it blends neighbors of the low resolution grid. Interpolation works with the flat surfaces. It does not work well with wavy or highly detailed surfaces that uses the bump map.*

The controls in the **Fast Glossy Interpolation** rollout can be used to interpolate reflections and refractions thus producing smooth results and improving rendering performance. The interpolation works by pre-calculating glossy reflections in a grid across the image. The number of rays shot by **mental ray** is governed by reflection **Glossy Samples** and refraction **Glossy Samples**.

Press Ctrl+S to save the scene.

Example 2: Creating the Chrome Material

Ok, now we have some knowledge of the Arch & Design material. Now, let's create the chrome material [see Figure 9].

Here's the process:

Open the **chromeMaterial_begin.max**. Apply an **Arch & Design** material to the teapot geometry in the scene. On the **Parameter Editor | Main material parameters rollout | Diffuse group**, set **Color** to **white**. Setting color to white will create a very highly reflective surface. On the **Reflection** group, set **Reflectivity** to **1**. Also, check **Metal material**. Now, take a test render.

Metal material allows you to define the reflection color using the **Diffuse** color parameter.

On the **Refraction** group, set **Color** to **Black** and set **IOR** to **25**.

The **Color** control on the **Refraction** group sets the color of the refraction. You can use this control to create the colored glass.

On the **BRDF** rollout, choose **By IOR (fresnel reflections)** and take a render [see Figure 9].

Save the scene with the name **chromeMaterial_end.max.**

Example 3: Creating the copper material
Now, let's create the different copper materials [see Figures 10, 14, and 21].

Let's start with the polished copper material.

Open the **archDefMat.max**. Save the scene with the name **copperMatEnd.max**. Apply an **Arch & Design** material to the teapot geometry in the scene. On the **Parameter Editor | Main material parameters rollout | Diffuse group**, set **Color** to the following RGB values: **0.592, 0.278**, and **0.165**. On the **Reflection** group, set **Reflectivity** to **1** and **Glossiness** to **0.9**. Also, check **Metal material**.

On the **Refraction** group, set **IOR** to **45**. On the **BRDF** rollout, choose **By IOR (fresnel reflections)** and take a render [see Figure 10].

Now, let's create the copper material with satin finish.

Apply a default **Arch & Design** material to the teapot in the scene. On the **Parameter Editor | Main material parameters rollout | Diffuse group**, set **Color** to the following RGB values: **0.592, 0.278**, and **0.165**. On the **Reflection** group, set **Reflectivity** to **0.8** and **Glossiness** to **0.5**. Also, check **Metal material**. Take a test render [see Figure 11]. You will see that the material is bright. You need to reduce the brightness of the material.

Set **Diffuse Level** to **0.3** to make the material less bright and take a test render. On the **Anisotropy** rollout, set **Anisotropy** to **0.05** to change the shape of the highlights and take a test render [see Figure 12].

F10   F11   F12

Anisotropy controls the shape of the highlight. At the value **1**, there will be no anisotropy and highlight will be round. At the value **0.01**, the highlight will be elongated. **Rotation** controls the orientation of the highlight. The values for **Rotation** ranges from **0** to **1**, **1** represents **360** degrees.

On the **Reflection** group, set **Glossy Samples** to **16** to increase the quality of the glossiness. On the **BRDF** rollout, set **0 deg. refl** to **0.9** and take a test render [see Figure 13]. Notice in the render that you need to reduce **Glossiness** value.

On the **Reflection** group, set **Glossiness** to **0.4**. On the **Fast Glossy Interpolation** rollout, set **Neighboring points to look up** to **8** and turn on **High detail distance**. Next, set distance to **1** for **High detail distance**. Now, take a test render [see Figure 14].

Neighboring points to look up lets you set the number of stored grid points are looked up to smooth out the reflective glossiness. The default value for this parameter is **2**. Higher values smear the glossiness. **High detail distance** allows **mental ray** to trace second set of rays to create a clearer version of the glossiness within the specified radius defined by this parameter.

Now, let's create the brushed copper material.

Apply a default **Arch & Design** material to the teapot in the scene. On the **Parameter Editor | Main material parameters rollout | Diffuse group**, set **Color** to the following RGB values: **0.592, 0.278**, and **0.165**. On the **Reflection** group, set **Reflectivity** to **0.5** and **Glossiness** to **0.5** as well. Also, check **Metal material**. Now, take a test render [see Figure 15].

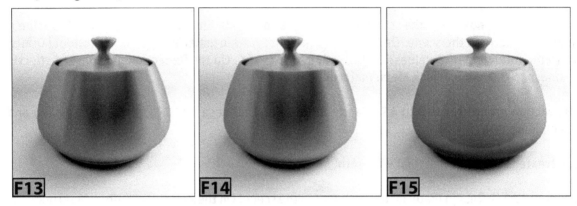

Now, we will use the **Noise** map to create brushed metal look in the reflections.

On the **Reflection** group, click **Color** button. On the **Material/Map Browser | Maps | Standard rollout**, double-click **Noise**. On the **Noise Parameters** rollout, set **Noise Type** as **Fractal** and set **Size** to **1** to create tiny dots in the noise pattern [see Figure 16]. On the **Coordinates** rollout, set **Source** to **Explicit Map Channel**. Also, set **V** and **W** to **100** in the **Tiling** column to create streaks in the noise pattern [see Figure 17].

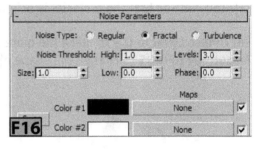

On the **Noise Parameters** rollout, set **Color #1** to medium gray and take a test render [see Figure 18]. On the material's **Refraction** group, set **IOR** to **45**. On the **BRDF** rollout, choose **By IOR (fresnel reflections)** and take a test render [see Figure 19]. On the **Anisotropy** rollout, set **Anisotropy** to **0.05** to change the shape of the highlights and take a test render [see Figure 20].

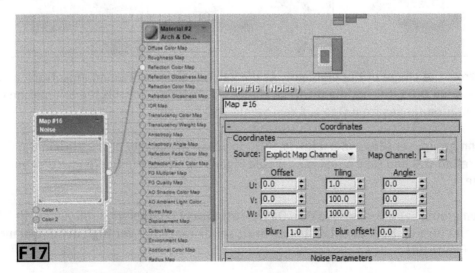

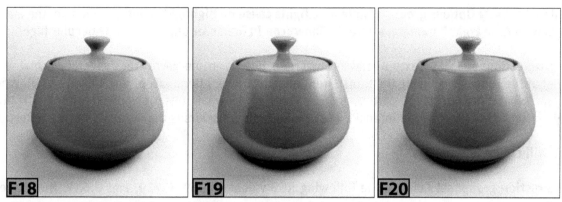
F18 F19 F20

Now, I will increase the reflectivity and glossiness values of the surface.

On the material's **Reflection** group, set **Reflectivity** and **Glossiness** to **0.8**. On the **Fast Glossy Interpolation** rollout, set **Interpolation grid density** to **1/4 (quarter resolution)**, **Neighboring points to look up** to **4**, and turn on **High detail distance**. Next, set distance to **2** for **High detail distance**. Now, take a render [see Figure 21]. Press **Ctrl+S** to save the scene.

Example 3: Creating glass/thin Plastic film Materials
In this example, we're going to create different glass and thin plastic film materials [see Figures 22, 23, 25, 27, 28, and 30]. Let's start with the clear glass material. This material is suitable for solid geometries with some thickness.

Here's the process:

Open the **archDefMat.max**. Save the scene with the name **glassMatEnd.max**. Apply an **Arch & Design** material to the teapot geometry in the scene. On the **Parameter Editor | Main material parameters rollout | Diffuse group**, set **Color** to **black**. On the **Reflection** group, set **Reflectivity** to **1**. On the **Refraction** group, set **Transparency** to **1** and **IOR** to **1.5**. On the **BRDF** rollout, choose **By IOR (fresnel reflections)** and take a render. On the **Advanced Rendering Options** rollout, set **Max Trace Depth** to **8** in the **Reflections** and **Refraction** groups. Take a test render [see Figure 22].

F21

F22

When the trace depth is equal to the value specified by the **Reflections group | Max Trace Depth control**, **mental ray** shows only highlights and emulated reflections created using **Final Gathering**. The material behaves as if **Highlights+FG** checked on the **Main material parameters rollout | Reflection** group.

Cutoff Threshold sets a threshold level at which reflections are rejected. The default value for this control is **0.01**. At this value, rays that contribute less than **1%** to the final pixel are ignored.
Max Distance allows you to limit the reflections to a certain distance. It helps in speeding up the rendering as **mental ray** does not include distant objects to glossy reflections. **Fade to end color** lets you fade the reflections to this color. This is suitable for indoor scenes. When this option is turned off, reflections fade to the environment color which is suitable for outdoor scenes.

The optimization settings for the refraction are almost identical to those for reflections. When the trace depth is equal to the value specified by the **Refraction group | Max Trace Depth control**, the material refracts black.

Advanced Reflectivity Options group | Visible area lights cause no Highlights control, when on, the **mental ray** area lights with **Area Light Parameters rollout | Show Icon In Renderer** on, creates no specular highlights.

When **Skip reflections on inside (except total internal reflection)** is on, **mental ray** retains total internal reflection [TIR]. Most of the reflections inside the transparent objects are very faint except few known as TIR. When this option is on, **mental ray** boosts the performance by ignoring the weak reflections but retaining TIRs. **Relative Intensity of Highlights** controls the intensity of specular highlights versus the intensity of true reflections.

Next, you will create tinted glass.

On the **Refraction** group, set **Color** to the following RGB values: **0.969**, **0.729**, and **0.659**. Now, take a test render [see Figure 23].

Next, you will create frosted glass.

On the **Refraction** group, set **Transparency** and **Glossiness** to **0.8** and take a test render [see Figure 24].

You will notice that you need to reduce the glossiness farther to make a believable frosted glass. If you reduce the **Glossiness** value, you need to increase samples to compensate. Set **Glossiness** and **Glossy Samples** to **0.5** and **16**, respectively, and take a test render [see Figure 25].

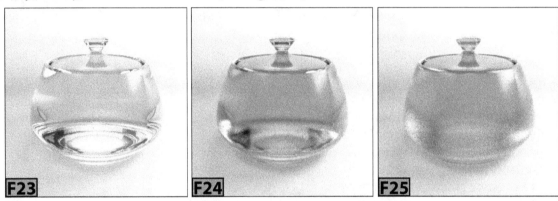

Now, the render is looking much better. Adding a little bit of translucency will make the effect much better so let's do it.

Turn on **Translucency** and set **Weight** to **0.2**. Change **Translucency Color** to the following RGB values: **0.969**, **0.729**, and **0.659** and then take a test render [see Figure 26].

Translucency is a special form of transparency. If you want a material to be translucent, there should exist some transparency in the material. The **Weight** parameter how much of the existing transparency is used as translucency. For example, if you set **Weight** to **0.3**, **30** percent of the transparency is used as translucency. It is best suited for thin walled objects such as windows panes or plastic films. **Color** controls the translucency color.

Note: Sub-surface Scattering
*You can create sub-surface scattering effects by using the glossy transparency with the translucency. However, the effect is not as good as created using the dedicated **SSS** shaders.*

On the **Diffuse** group, set **Diffuse Level** to **0.52** to reduce the brightness of the material. Press **Ctrl+S** to save the file.

Next, you will create a glass material that does not include any refraction. This glass is ideal for windows panes with single face.

Open **thinGlass_strat.max**. Apply an **Arch & Design** material to the plane geometry in the scene. On the **Parameter Editor | Main material parameters rollout | Diffuse group**, set **Color** to black. On the **Reflection** group, set **Reflectivity** to **1**. On the **Refraction** group, set **Transparency** to **1** and **IOR** to **1.5**. On the **BRDF** rollout, choose **By IOR (fresnel reflections)** and take a render.

On the **Refraction** group, set **Color** to the following RGB values: **0.737, 0.776**, and **0.98**. On the **Advanced Rendering Options** rollout, set **Max Trace Depth** to **8** in the **Reflection** and **Refraction** groups.   On the **Advanced Transparency Options** rollout, choose **Thin-walled (can use single face)** for **Glass / Translucency treat objects as**. Now, take a render [see Figure 27].

When you choose **Thin-walled (can use single face)**, the object behaves as if it is made of a very thin sheet of transparent material. On the other hand, **Solid (requires two sides on every object)** tells **mental ray** that the object is made of a solid, transparent substance.

Back Face Culling makes the surfaces invisible to the camera when seen from the reverse side. You can use this option to create magic walls. If you create walls of a room using planes with the normal facing inwards, you can render room from outside. The camera will see into the room, but the wall will still exists and behave normally. For example, they will cast shadows, photon will be bounced off them.

When you turn off **Transparency propagates Alpha channel**, the transparent objects have an opaque alpha. When on, the alpha-channel information is passed on to the background. The refraction and other transparency effects propagate the alpha of the background "through" the transparent object.

The two parameters in the **Indirect Illumination Options** group are multipliers. **FG/GI multiplier** lets you adjust the material response to the indirect light. **FG Quality** is a local multiplier for the number of final gather rays shot by the material.

Next, you will create a thin blurry plastic material.

Apply the default **Arch & Design** material to the plane geometry in the scene. On the **Parameter Editor | Main material parameters rollout | Diffuse group**, set **Color** to white. On the **Reflection** group, set **Reflectivity** to **1**. On the **Refraction** group, set **Transparency** to **0.9**, **Glossiness** to **0.6**, **Glossy Samples** to **16**, and **IOR** to **1.5**. On the **BRDF** rollout, choose **By IOR (fresnel reflections)**.

On the **Advanced Transparency Options** group, choose **Thin-walled (can use single face)** option for **Glass / Translucency** treat objects as. Also, turn on **Transparency propagates Alpha channel** and then take a render [see Figure 28].

If you want to create strong blur, adjust the values of **Transparency** and **Glossiness** in the **Refraction** group. Also, enable **Translucency**.

On the **Refraction** group, set **Transparency** to **0.8**, **Glossiness** to **0.8**, and **Glossy Samples** to **16**. Check **Translucency** and set **Weight** to **0.2** and then take a render [see Figure 29].

Save the scene with the name **thinGlass_End.max**.

Example 4: Creating the water material
In this example, we are going to create the water material [see Figure 32].

Here's the process:

Open the **archDefMat.max**. Apply an **Arch & Design** material to the teapot geometry in the scene. On the **Parameter Editor | Main material parameters rollout | Diffuse group**, set **Color** to the following RGB values: **0.0, 0.058**, and **0.019**. On the **Reflection** group, set **Reflectivity** to **1**. On the **Refraction** group, set **IOR** to **1.3**. On the **BRDF** rollout, choose **By IOR (fresnel reflections)**. Now, take a test render [see Figure 30].

On the **Special Purpose Maps** rollout of the material, set **Bump** to **0.1** and then click **Bump's None** button. On the **Material/Map Browser | Maps | mental ray rollout**, double-click **Ocean**. Take a test render [see Figure 31].

You need to adjust the values for ocean parameters to get a nice bump.

On the **Ocean Parameters** rollout, set **Largest** to **0.5**, **Smallest** to **0.25**, **Quantity** to **3**, and **Steepness** to **1** and then take a render [see Figure 32].

Save the scene with the name **waterMat_End.max**.

Example 5: Creating the Sofa Fabric Material
In this example, we're going to create the sofa fabric material [see Figure 33].

Here's the process:

Open the **archDefMat.max**. Apply an **Arch & Design** material to the teapot geometry in the scene. Rename the material as **sofaFabricMat**. On the **Main material parameters** rollout, click **Color's** button. On the **Material/Map Browser | Maps | Standard rollout**, double-click **Bitmap**. On the **Select Bitmap Image File** dialog, choose **sofaFabricDif.jpg**.

On the **Coordinates** rollout, set **U** and **V** to **2** in **Tiling** column. Also, set **Blur** to **0.2**. On the **Parameter Editor | Main material parameters rollout | Reflection group**, set **Reflectivity** to **0.08**, **Glossiness** to **0.5**, and **Glossy Samples** to **32**. On the **BRDF** rollout, set **0 deg. refl** to **1**. On the **Special Purpose Maps** rollout of the material, click **Bump's None** button. On the **Material/Map Browser | Maps | Standard rollout**, double-click **Bitmap**. On the **Select Bitmap Image File** dialog, choose **sofaFabricBump.jpg**.

On the **Coordinates** rollout, set **U** and **V** to **2** in **Tiling** column. Also, set **Blur** to **0.2**. On the **Special Purpose Maps** rollout of the material, set **Bump** to **0.4** and take a render [see Figure 33].

Save the scene with the name **sofaMat_End.max**.

Example 6: Creating the wood cabinet material
In this example, we are going to create the wood cabinet material [see Figure 34].

Open the **archDefMat.max**. Apply an **Arch & Design** material to the teapot geometry in the scene. Rename the material as **woodCabinetMat**. On the **Main material parameters rollout | Diffuse group**, click **Color's** button. On the **Material/Map Browser | Maps | Standard rollout**, double-click **Bitmap**.

On the **Select Bitmap Image File** dialog, choose **woodCabinetDiff.png**. On the **Coordinates** rollout, set **U** and **V** to **2** in **Tiling** column. Also, set **Blur** to **0.2**. On the **Parameter Editor | Main material parameters rollout | Reflection group**, set **Reflectivity** to **0.4**, **Glossiness** to **0.7**, and **Glossy Samples** to **32**. On the **Main material parameters rollout | Reflection group**, click **Glossiness** button. On the **Material/Map Browser | Maps | Standard rollout**, double-click **Bitmap**.

On the **Select Bitmap Image File** dialog, choose **woodCabinetGloss.png**. On the **Coordinates** rollout, set **U** and **V** to **2** in **Tiling** column. Also, set **Blur** to **0.2**. Now, take a test render. On the **Special Purpose Maps** rollout of the material, click **Bump's None** button. On the **Material/Map Browser | Maps | Standard rollout**, double-click **Bitmap**. On the **Select Bitmap Image File** dialog, choose **woodCabinetBump.png**.

Take a render [see Figure 34]. Save the scene with the name **wood_Cabinet.max**.

Example 7: Creating the parquet material
In this example, we're going to create parquet material for the floor [see Figure 35].

F33   F34   F35

Here's the process:

Open the **archDefMat.max**. Apply an **Arch & Design** material to the teapot geometry in the scene. Rename the material as **woodParquetMat**. On the **Main material parameters rollout | Diffuse group**, click **Color's** button. On the **Material/Map Browser | Maps | Standard rollout**, double-click **Bitmap**. On the **Select Bitmap Image File** dialog, choose **floorParquetDiff.png**.

On the **Coordinates** rollout, set **U** and **V** to **2** in **Tiling** column. Also, set **Blur** to **0.2**. On the **Parameter Editor | Main material parameters rollout | Reflection group**, set **Reflectivity** to **0.7**, **Glossiness** to **0.7**, and **Glossy Samples** to **16**. On the **Main material parameters rollout | Reflection group**, click **Color's** button. On the **Material/Map Browser | Maps | Standard rollout**, double-click **Bitmap**. On the **Select Bitmap Image File** dialog, choose **floorParquetRef.png**. On the **Coordinates** rollout, set **U** and **V** to **2** in **Tiling** column. Also, set **Blur** to **0.2**.

On the **Special Purpose Maps** rollout of the material, click **Bump's None** button. On the **Material/Map Browser | Maps | Standard rollout**, double-click **Bitmap**. On the **Select Bitmap Image File** dialog, choose **floorParquetBump. png**. On the **Coordinates** rollout, turn off **Use Real-World Scale**. Set **U** and **V** to **2** in **Tiling** column. Also, set **Blur** to **0.2**. On the **Special Purpose Maps** rollout of the material, set **Bump** to **0.4** and take a render [see Figure 35].

Save the scene with the name **parquetMat_End.max**.

The Last Word

In this section, I described the **Arch & Design** material. This material is a monolithic material designed to support most of the material that you will use in the architectural and product design renderings. This material is highly tuned for modeling fast glossy reflective and refractive surfaces.

Other eBooks from Raavi Design

Raavi O'Connor

Build Studio Light Setup
Using
3ds Max and VRay

raavidesign.blogspot.co.uk

Raavi O'Connor

Exploring
Standard Materials
in 3ds Max 2015

raavidesign.blogspot.co.uk

Raavi O'Connor

Create
Backgrounds, Textures, and Maps
In Photoshop
Using Photoshop CC 2014

raavidesign.blogspot.co.uk

Raavi O'Connor

Exploring
Utilities Nodes
In Maya 2016

raavidesign.blogspot.co.uk

b-2   Other eBooks by Raavi Design

Raavi O'Connor

Beginner's Guide To Mental Ray and Autodesk Materials In 3ds Max 2016

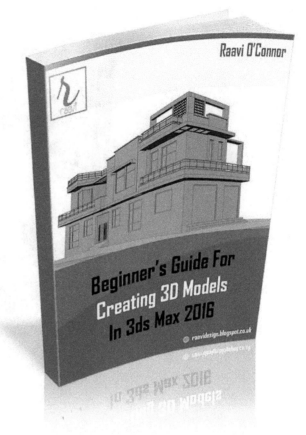

Raavi O'Connor

Beginner's Guide For Creating 3D Models In 3ds Max 2016